IMAGES
of America

SYRACUSE AND LAKE WAWASEE

ELKHART COUNTY

MAXWELTON
GOLF COURSE

BONER
LAKE

LAKE WAWASEE

SYRACUSE
LAKE

SYRACUSE

B. & O.

R.R. WILLOW GROVE

SARGENT'S
HOTEL

WAWASEE P.O.

GOLF

COURSE

SPINK-
WAWASEE
HOTEL

JOHNSON
BAY

B. & O. R.

ROUTE 13
PICKWICK PARK
KALE ISLAND
CONKLIN BAY
HOTEL
OAKWOOD

MARINE
STATION

BLACK
POINT

BRUNJES
PARK

ROUTE 13

THE
TAVERN

WACO
DANCE
PAVILLION

CRO
NES
HOT

IDEAL
BEACH

SOUTH SHORE
HOTEL

SOUTH SHORE
GOLF COURSE

VAWTER
PARK

HIGHLAND
VIEW
GARDENS

TURK
CREE
GOLF CO

STAT
FISH
HATCH

ROUTE 13

JOHNSON'S
HOTEL

ELMWOOD HEIGHTS

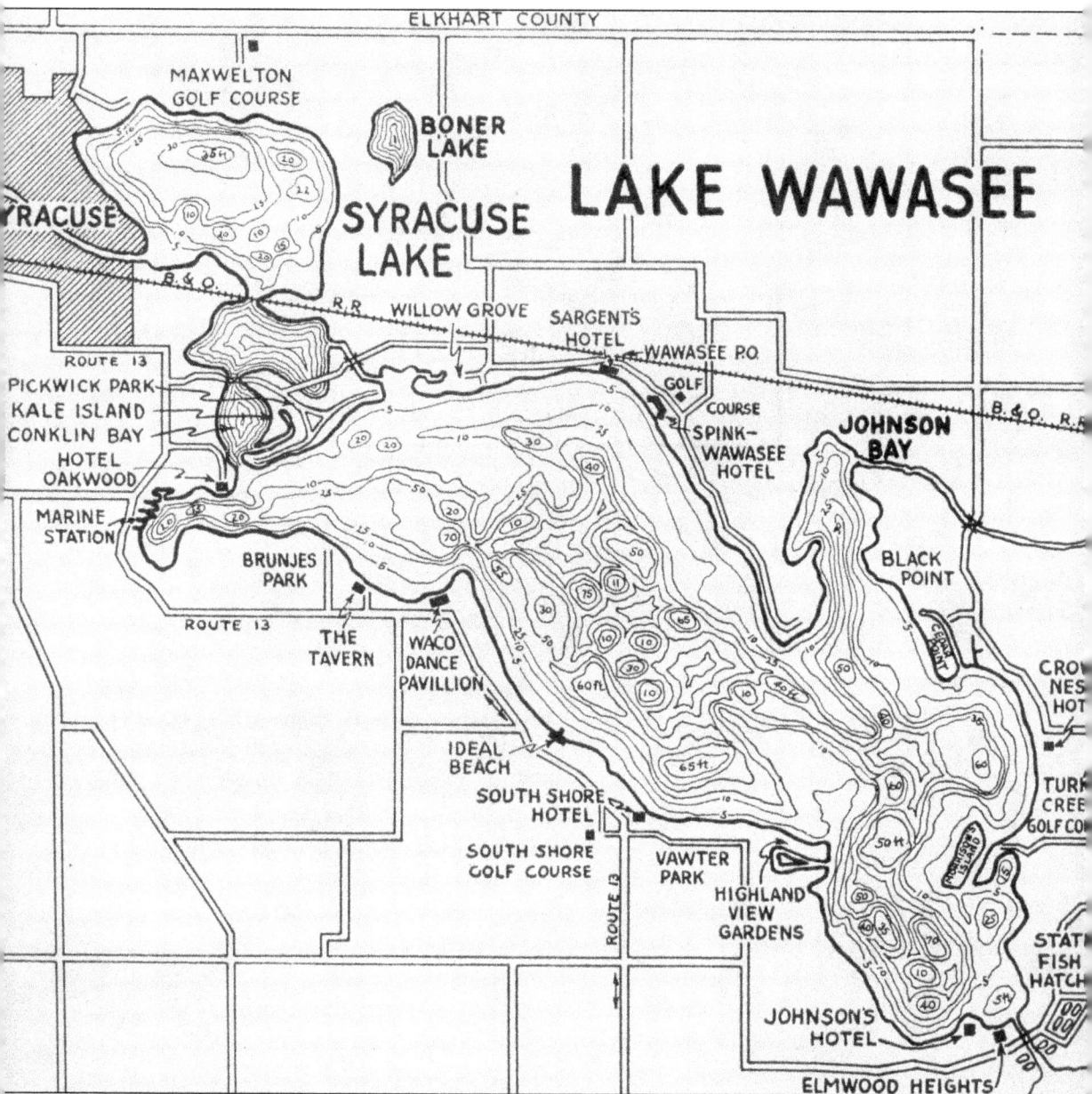

This map from a 1930s lake area guide shows the neighborhoods and prominent hotels of the day. (Courtesy of the Syracuse-Wawasee Historical Museum.)

IMAGES
of America

SYRACUSE AND LAKE WAWASEE

Erin Lomax and Ann Vanderford Garceau

ARCADIA
PUBLISHING

Published by Arcadia Publishing
Charleston, South Carolina

Library of Congress Control Number: 2013951435

For all general information, please contact Arcadia Publishing:
Telephone 843-853-2070
Fax 843-853-0044
E-mail sales@arcadiapublishing.com
For customer service and orders:
Toll-Free 1-888-313-2665

Visit us on the Internet at www.arcadiapublishing.com

Erin dedicates this book to the memory of her grandparents, Jim and Pat Breen, who both spent many happy days on the lakes.

Ann dedicates this book to her family. Her great-grandmother and grandparents first came to Lake Wawasee around 1910 on the B&O Railroad and traveled by launch to Morrison Island. Her father, Jack Vanderford, grew up on Sand Point in the 1920s and 1930s, returning after World War II to raise his family on the lake, becoming a businessman in the community and secretary-treasurer of the Wawasee Property Owners Association for 25 years. With this book, Ann hopes to capture precious memories of a time gone by for her descendants and the community.

CONTENTS

Acknowledgments   6

Introduction   7

1.   Foundations of Community Life   9

2.   Hotels and Restaurants   43

3.   Boats and Marinas   67

4.   Neighborhoods and Islands   83

5.   Pastimes, Celebrations, and Service   103

Bibliography   127

ACKNOWLEDGMENTS

The authors wish to thank numerous individuals from the area for their assistance in completing this book. The board of directors of the Syracuse-Wawasee Historical Museum has been supportive of our project since its inception, and has been unwaveringly generous in allowing us to use images housed in their collection. In particular, we wish to thank Karen Kelsheimer, director of the Syracuse-Wawasee Historical Museum, for her outstanding assistance with this project. Unless otherwise noted, all images in this book are courtesy of the Syracuse-Wawasee Historical Museum.

We wish to recognize the generous contributions of family photographs and postcard collections from Garry Ringler, Dave Sheets, Chris Harris, Byron Connolly, the Garceau family, and the Breen family. We also wish to thank the numerous area residents who responded to our inquiries as we researched the history of the Syracuse-Wawasee area.

We stand on the shoulders of the historians and local citizens whose dedication led them to preserve Syracuse and Lake Wawasee history, either through the written word, photographic work, or simply through their memories of a time gone by. Among many, the authors wish to acknowledge the work and words of Ron and Steve Sharp, Jack Elam, George Miles, C.C. Bachman, the editors of the *Syracuse Journal* and the *Mail-Journal* newspapers, the Syracuse Public Library, the descendants of Nathaniel Crow, the Hirschman family, Ken Harkless, the Sudlow family, J.P. Dolan, Debbie Blackwell Smith, Scott Edgell, Bill Spurgeon, Eli Lilly, and various area authors. Special thanks also to Jack Vanderford, Jack Teetor, area "breakfast clubs," and the participants of the 1993 Spurgeon audio interviews, for their wonderful oral history contributions. Last, but certainly not least, the authors wish to thank their families and friends for their support.

To everyone who helped us, and to anyone we may have missed, thank you. Your dedication to local history is what keeps it alive. We welcome documented corrections and additions, which can be directed to the authors via the Syracuse-Wawasee Historical Museum.

The Syracuse-Wawasee Historical Museum, located in the Syracuse Community Center, was founded after the community's sesquicentennial celebration in 1987. The museum's mission is to preserve objects from families and businesses of the area, make them available for viewing, and provide programs so that visitors and future generations may have a better understanding of the people and events that have made our community what it is today.

INTRODUCTION

Located in the northeastern corner of Indiana, Syracuse and its lakes provide residents and seasonal visitors alike endless opportunities to make lifelong memories thanks to the natural beauty of the area, which continues to attract successive generations of families. Lakes Wawasee and Syracuse lie just north of the St. Lawrence continental divide, meaning their waters are part of the Great Lakes watershed and eventually flow to the Atlantic Ocean. During the last glaciation of the Wisconsin Ice Age, the Syracuse-Wawasee area lay under a massive glacier that blanketed most of Canada, New England, and the upper Midwest and extended into sections of what would become the Pacific Northwest. The glacier's retreat, in approximately 10,000 BC, formed the basin of Lake Wawasee and Syracuse Lake, as well as nearly 400 other lakes in Indiana. Lake Wawasee and Syracuse Lake are connected by a channel. Lake Wawasee is the largest natural lake in Indiana, with an average depth of 22 feet—it is 77 feet at its deepest—and an approximate size of over 3,000 acres. Originating in neighboring Noble County, Turkey Creek flows through several small lakes before entering Lake Wawasee at the southeast end. After flowing through the channel and Syracuse Lake, it exits near Henry Ward Park, going over the dam spillway and meandering in a northwesterly direction before emptying into the Elkhart River at Goshen Pond. The Indiana Department of Statistics and Geology reported in 1901 that if the levels of Lake Wawasee were dropped by 40 feet, it would create four separate, unconnected bodies of water.

Nomadic Paleo-Indians, the earliest Native Americans, began to occupy the land that became Indiana at the end of the last glaciation. Numerous artifacts of prehistoric cultures have been recovered locally. The historic period began around 1650 AD, when European explorers began recording their experiences of contact with area natives. When Indiana became a state in 1816, the northern section was occupied by the Miami and Pottawatomi tribes. At the time of the first white settlers, the politically powerful leader of the Miami tribe in this region was Chief Papakeecha, also known as Flat Belly (seemingly a euphemistic name as he aged), who claimed to have fought in the Battle of Tippecanoe. According to historical accounts, Flat Belly was 60 years old in the 1830s and was a large, strong man of dark, copper color weighing approximately 300 pounds. His brother was Wa-wa-aus-see, Lake Wawasee's namesake. In the 1826 Indian Treaty of Mississinewa, the Miami agreed to cede the bulk of Miami lands in northern Indiana to the United States. By the 1830s, Papakeecha was living on a 36-square-mile reservation in a house; by 1834, the house had been destroyed in a storm and the land, by treaty, was relinquished to the federal government. The Native American removal began at this point. Papakeecha died in approximately 1837, although some sources cite his death as late as 1840.

In its early days, Syracuse was somewhat of a rough-and-tumble town on the edges of civilization, one that didn't have any local law enforcement officers for the first several decades of its existence. The Indiana Territory, created in 1800, was the first new territory carved from the lands of the Northwest Territory, which was organized in 1787. In the first few decades of the 19th century, the federal government proclaimed the Indiana Territory to be nearly free of its native inhabitants. In the 1830s, so many young settlers were attracted to free land in Kosciusko County that there was a land rush. According to Waldo Adams, first vice-president of the Kosciusko County Historical Society, "would-be settlers waited on the Elkhart-Kosciusko County border, near the eastern end of Goshen to run for their stakes."

Syracuse town founders Henry Ward and Samuel Crosson (sometimes spelled "Crawson" in early documents) settled in the area in 1832 and built a dam across Turkey Creek to power a mill that they constructed. It was the first recorded commercial enterprise in Syracuse history. Huntington Road, part of what is now Huntington Street and State Road 13 (SR 13), was surveyed and created in 1834. The township was incorporated in June 1836, and the community soon included a schoolhouse, general store, public house, blacksmith, tannery, shoemaker, carpenter, and other merchants. The Church of God became active in the township as early as 1856. By 1858, elder George Thomas established the Lake Bethel Church on the east side of Lake Wawasee. The growing congregation dedicated a new church building near downtown Syracuse on October 13, 1867, and continues to worship there today. Syracuse was incorporated in October 1876.

In its heyday, the Baltimore & Ohio Railroad (B&O) stretched from Staten Island in New York all the way into Illinois. In 1874, the town of Syracuse became part of its line, allowing easier transport of goods and people. The town's economy began to flourish. The area's natural beauty attracted tourists, and eventually seasonal visitors, who built homes on the lake. With the population increase of both seasonal and permanent residents, merchants and restaurants saw to the town's material and entertainment needs. Syracuse became known for its marl and concrete, of which many thousands of barrels per day were produced at the town's Sandusky Portland Cement Company. Schools and churches were plentiful in this idyllic town in northeastern Indiana.

George W. Miles, commissioner of fisheries and game for Indiana, gives this charmingly evocative description of Syracuse in his biennial report for 1913–1914:

> And a pretty little town [Syracuse is] indeed, with its shady streets, and its roofs and steeples reaching above the trees amidst which it nestles. Along the shore at the town is a row of boathouses, which cast their long reflection in the water on a calm day and thus heighten the scene from the lake. Not a more beautiful view is to be met with anywhere than when one has passed beneath the railway bridge and is coming into the lake as he faces town, directly west. Let it be evening and sunset time, when the lake is like Poe's dank tarn of Aubur that lay in unruffled lustre. Then there will be two towns, one upside down beneath the other, with their hills, [tree]-tops and spires brought boldly into relief by the purple and orange masses of light surrounding the golden red sun.

This book is meant to represent a snapshot through the 1940s of the long and storied history of a town and its lakes, which are much beloved by many from all walks of life and from all over the world. Like any snapshot, it cannot possibly hope to include everything. The photographic legacy left by previous generations allows us to peek briefly into their world. The images themselves weave the history of Syracuse through all of its triumphs and tragedies—and through the people who shaped them.

One

FOUNDATIONS OF COMMUNITY LIFE

Before the 1870s, the Syracuse area was home to mainly farmers and merchants. Many of them had not started their lives in northern Indiana, but rather had traveled from other parts of the United States or abroad and found opportunity in the area. This mixture was not unusual for small Midwestern towns at the time; however, in 1874, Syracuse was fortunate to have the Baltimore & Ohio Railroad reach town. The railroad provided freight service for the community's industries and brought new residents as well as vacationers.

With an influx of people brought in by the railroad, Syracuse began to grow. Several churches were established, along with hotels, restaurants, marinas, mercantile stores, factories, and new homes. The schools enjoyed a well-deserved reputation for excellence. A circulating library that rented books for a fee became available in 1886 and had about 40 subscribers; the first public library in Syracuse was established in 1909. Chautauqua events also brought entertainment and culture to the town.

Main Street became a vibrant area for both commerce and socialization, as stores catered to those of all walks of life. Weekly street concerts on a raised bandstand in the summertime brought everyone in town together for fun and dancing. As the town grew, so did its economy, its population, and the opportunity to newcomers for a better life.

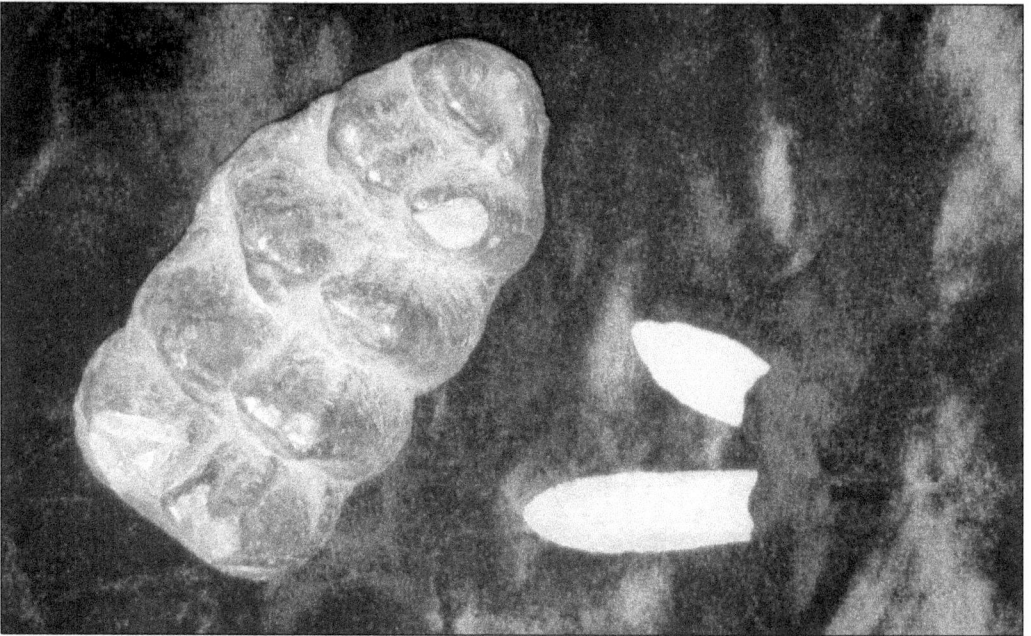

Remnants of extinct Ice Age animals have been found near Syracuse. In the 1930s, a complete skeleton of a mastodon was unearthed at the Charles Fledheiser farm, southeast of Cromwell, by the Buffalo Museum of Science and Natural History of New York. The massive mastodon tooth (left) in this photograph was discovered in the marl of Waubee Lake in 1918 by Clifford Foster. The fluted Clovis points (right) were used in hunting these large animals.

Cedar Point, on the east side of Lake Wawasee, is a glacial kame created during the most recent ice age. Evidence of trade among local Paleo-Indians was discovered in the form of shell items originating from the Gulf of Mexico area. Human remains of native inhabitants were also found when the hill began to be altered in the 1880s to build some of Wawasee's earliest homes. (Courtesy of Dave Sheets.)

Indian Hill, Syracuse Lake, Syracuse, Ind.   32719-r

A prominent landscape feature on the north shore of Syracuse Lake, Indian Hill is so named because the native tribes of the area may have wrapped their dead in cloth and secured them among tree branches. Early settlers evidently found the bones on the ground once the cloth had disintegrated. Legends of ceremonial dances and evidence of toolmaking were substantiated when artifacts were discovered in the hill in the 1800s. (Courtesy of Chris Harris.)

In the summer of 1959, a Native American dugout canoe was recovered from its resting place in Syracuse Lake by Ed Jamison and his son Richard. An investigation showed that the canoe was made out of a single large yellow poplar tree. Hatchet marks from shaping the log remained visible on the outside, as well as the charred effects of the burning-out process used to hollow out the inside of the canoe.

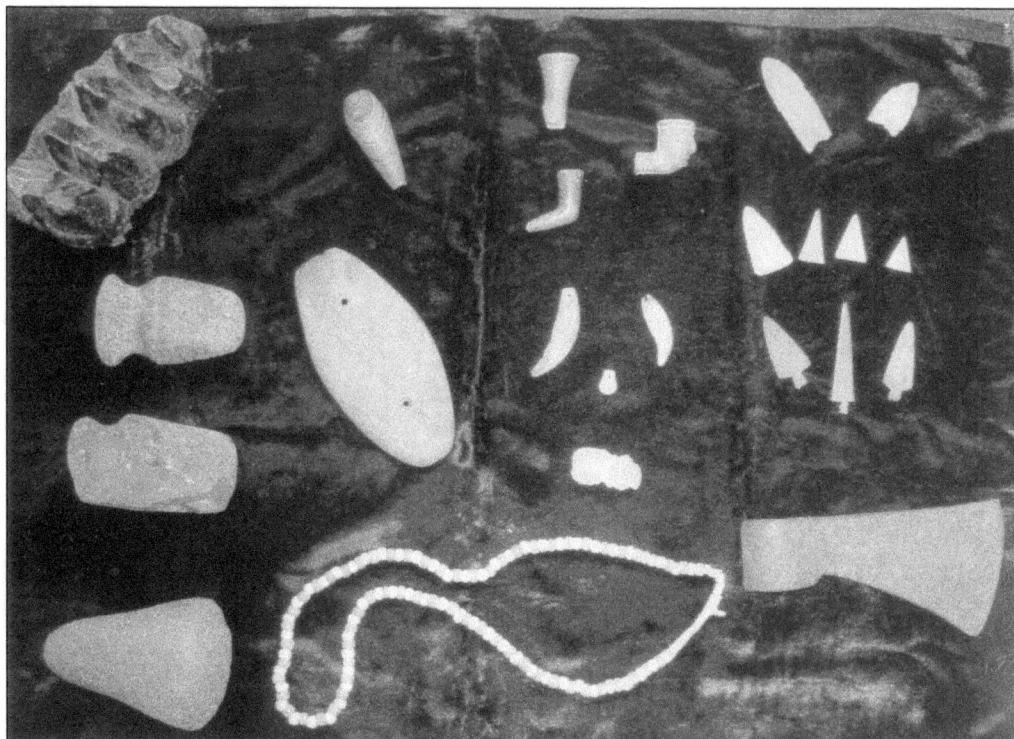

Hundreds of artifacts crafted by Native Americans have been unearthed in the Syracuse area over the years, some of which are pictured above. One of the best-known collections of artifacts belonged to J.P. Dolan (left), a Syracuse educator and influential citizen. In the mid-1930s, Eli Lilly was so enraptured by the artifacts in Dolan's "Indian Cabinet" that a lifelong passion for Midwestern archaeology was ignited. This passion led Lilly to establish anthropology fellowships at several universities, publish his book *Prehistoric Antiquities of Indiana*, and provide funds through the Indiana Historical Society to purchase Angel Mounds, an important prehistoric site in southern Indiana that the state took title of in 1946. With Lilly's continued support, a formal department of anthropology was created at Indiana University in 1947, and the Glenn Black Laboratory of Archaeology was dedicated on campus in 1971.

Henry Ward and Samuel Crosson, two founders of Syracuse, built a dam to run their gristmill on Turkey Creek. Nearby farmers would travel to Syracuse to use the mill's services. Around 1837 the mill was washed away, contributing to Ward and Crosson's eventual financial ruin. The dam seen here was built after the original dam washed away; the mill race was filled in after many years to become Dolan Drive.

Built for the arrival of the Baltimore & Ohio Railroad (B&O), this depot was active from 1874 through 1916. It remained in use until being moved off the property in 1957. H.W. Buchholz, a B&O agent from the 1890s through 1937, stands to the left with his son Ernest beside him on the baggage wagon. After graduating from high school in 1916, Ernest Buchholz became a career employee with the railroad. (Courtesy of Garry Ringler.)

13

This Prairie-style brick depot was constructed around 1916 and stood until 2013, when it was demolished after having been on the Indiana Landmarks Ten Most Endangered Buildings list for several years. Ernest Buchholz, the stationmaster and Syracuse clerk-treasurer, stands proudly in front of the depot in this 1930s photograph.

Built in the early 1900s, another B&O station, seen here in the 1920s, was located just north of Cedar Beach. For 50 years, the station handled much of the summer tourist traffic to Lake Wawasee. Closed in 1947, the building was moved to property just east of Benton, Indiana, in 1950. It still stands today on Highway 33. (Courtesy of Garry Ringler.)

14

Before refrigeration, lake ice was harvested and stored for use in warmer months. Blocks of ice were pulled by horses to icehouses like this one on Medusa Street, owned by the Disher family. Packed in sawdust created by a nearby factory, blocks of ice were used locally or shipped by rail as far as Chicago—up to 35 carloads per day around 1900.

The Harkless Garage sat near Syracuse Lake on the far eastern end of Main Street. Sheldon Harkless was a machinist, and his descendants inherited his artistic and mechanical talents. His son Ken worked with boats and preserved local history through sketches and paintings, as did Sheldon's granddaughter Betty Harkless Appenzeller. Her sons Jan and Patrick continue the tradition today through the high-quality restoration of antique automobiles.

In 1899, Arthur Newberry, one of the founders of the Sandusky Portland Cement Company of Sandusky, Ohio, scouted a large deposit of marl in the Syracuse lakes area that was capable of supplying 2,500 pounds of marl a day for 200 years. Marl was the main component in Portland cement, and since the Chicago market was only 110 miles by rail from Syracuse, the company built a cement plant on Medusa Street in Syracuse at a cost of $366,000. The plant is seen above during its heyday, when it employed upwards of 150 workers and produced 600 barrels of concrete a day using the enormous machines pictured below.

The plant owned substantial acreage along the B&O tracks at the east end of Medusa Street to export materials out of Syracuse.

The employees of the cement company pose with a massive, continuously revolving kiln used to incinerate the clay-like marl that created quicklime, which was then cooled and packaged for cement and mortar.

Built in 1907 for the transport of marl and clay, the Syracuse & Milford Railway, also called the Mud Line, was comprised of six miles of track that ran from just east of Syracuse, south to Oak Park and the western edge of Wawasee, and then west-southwest to Waubee Lake, where it met up with the Cleveland, Cincinnati, Chicago & St. Louis Railway near Milford. It was dismantled in 1923.

THE MADUCA DREDGE, SYRACUSE, IND.

The Medusa Dredge, the largest dredge ever launched on a lake in Indiana, mined marl out of Wawasee. It cost $25,000 to construct in 1907 and supplied the cement plant in Syracuse with marl until the outbreak of World War I. By 1920, the lake was becoming residential, extensive marl mining was frowned upon, and limestone began to be used to make cement, causing the plant to be abandoned shortly thereafter.

Tugs like this one, which is possibly the *Spencer B.*, were used to move barges loaded with marl to the slip, where the marl was offloaded into small railcars to be transported to the cement plant.

In the early 1910s, Indiana was seeking locations for fish hatcheries. The Northern Indiana Improvement Company, with Charles Sudlow as president, had recently dammed Lake Papakeechie. When George Miles, a resident of Syracuse and the state commissioner of fisheries and game, approached Sudlow, the company gave the state a perpetual lease on the ground between the two lakes, creating the Wawasee State Fish Hatchery in 1912. (Courtesy of Garry Ringler.)

On the summit of the large hill to the west overlooking the Wawasee State Fish Hatchery, a large residence was erected for the custodian that also provided temporary lodging for visiting deputies and wardens. The terraces were created when the hill's gravel was used to construct the embankments for the rearing ponds. (Courtesy of Chris Harris.)

In 1895, Indiana University established a "biological station" on Wawasee, and was involved in hydrographic mapping and depth measurements of the lakes. Instruction and research went on for four summers until 1898, when the station was abandoned. The structure was dismantled and its materials were used to build two small bungalows in Vawter Park. The research station was moved to Winona Lake. (Courtesy of Wylie House Museum, Indiana University.)

One of the earliest known photographs of Main Street in Syracuse, looking east towards Syracuse Lake, shows it as a dirt road in 1870. The building on the right is possibly the one that still stands on the corner of Main and Huntington Streets.

Seen here in 1886, the Harkless Tin Shop stood on a now-vacated street just south of East Main Street. The structure was later moved to become part of the Harkless Garage. From left to right are Charles Smith, Sheldon Harkless, Jim Lewis, Mrs. J.A. Harkless, Sam Snavely, Mabel Brady, Harry Howard, Ada Brady, Winnie Holloway, May Holloway, and A.M. Jones.

A hardware store has been at the same site on West Main Street in Syracuse for around 100 years. Ross Osborn purchased an established hardware store in 1922 and ran it through the mid-1940s. Helpful managers of the renamed Syracuse Hardware included Floyd Disher and Everett Crow; Harry Coy was a clerk for years. Art Carboneau, who took over in 1969, still serves the community today. (Courtesy of the Carboneau family.)

Bushong's Barber Shop was the oldest continually operated family business in Syracuse at one time. Civil War veteran Elias "Eli" Bushong (right) started barbering soon after returning from the war. The shop (pictured here), built around 1900, featured the town's first and largest plate glass window. Bushong's sons Bill (left) and Vern (center), along with his grandson Joe, turned over the shears one last time in 1959 to great-grandson George. (Courtesy of Garry Ringler.)

Klink's Meat Market, seen here in the early 1900s, sold freshly butchered local meat to Syracuse residents. Klink's served the community for decades and eventually became a full-service grocery located in the Wawasee Village. (Courtesy of Garry Ringler.)

The Star Clothing Store was established in downtown Syracuse by W.G. Connolly in 1902. It moved to the Connolly Building in 1928. Byron Connolly, seen here as a young man, became a Syracuse grocer. He delighted in sharing the postcard collection he kept in his "postcard box" with customers. That same box became the heart of the Syracuse-Wawasee Historical Museum's postcard collection.

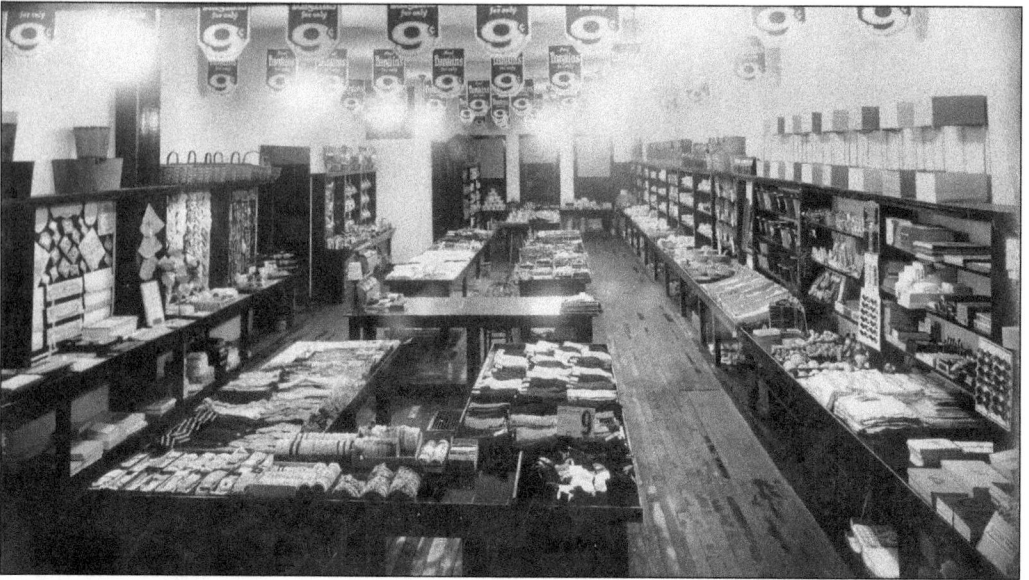

The interior of the Star Clothing Store shows an impressive array of menswear and items for women and children. Both locals and summer vacationers frequented the store, which survived well into the 1960s. The building, which included a neighboring variety store, was torn down around 1987. Today, a parking lot is in its place.

Silas L. Ketring constructed this building in 1900. It was used as a jewelry store, post office, and several drugstores with offices upstairs before Ralph E. and Blanche Thornburg began their drugstore in 1915, starting what would become one of the oldest family-owned retail businesses in Syracuse. They absorbed the jewelry store next door and sold jewelry, silverware, and phonographs.

Ralph E. Thornburg (right) partnered with Charles "Jim" Kroh in 1924. As time went on, their sons and grandsons also entered the business. In 1948 it was moved to the Pickwick Block, and later to the Wawasee Village. Ralph's friendly manner of greeting customers and his cheery "Hurry back!" to everyone as they left the store made people happy to come in.

Thornburg's Drugstore was a popular meeting spot in town for both locals and visitors. Boaters would dock at the public pier and make the short walk uptown for Thornburg's wide selection of soda fountain treats and snacks. The store made its own chocolate syrup. They were famous for their chocolate pecan sundaes and fountain drinks. Nellie Mann (Laughlin) is seen here dipping ice cream cones. (Courtesy of Chris Harris.)

This 1940s photograph shows an updated façade on the Ketring Building. Thornburg's Drug Store occupied the ground floor. Its windows were decorated at Halloween with scenes painted by local students. The Syracuse Lodge No. 454 Free and Accepted Masons moved its meetings to the building's second floor in 1945, eventually buying and remodeling it. In 1873, the building's namesake, Silas L. Ketring, was the first senior warden of the lodge.

In 1905, before the appearance of automobiles, horse-drawn vehicles line Main Street in this view to the west. Notice the sidewalks and pedestrian crosswalks, even though the streets are not paved. The first building on the left, the longtime home of a dime store and the Star Clothing Store, was later razed to make room for a parking lot. The Ketring Building is on the right.

When Dot and Dee Stiver purchased this filling station on the original State Road 13 near what is now Lakeside Park in Syracuse, they physically shifted the building to a different angle. In the 1930s, those who came to Lake Wawasee to gamble often stopped at the station for gas.

Auer's Friendly Service, seen here in the 1950s, was owned by John Auer (right) and his son Nelson (center). They ran it as a full-service Mobil gas station. Their wrecker service came to the aid of many a vehicle, even tractor-trailers on nearby Route 6. In the late 1950s or early 1960s, Auer's expanded to include auto supply parts. (Courtesy of Garry Ringler.)

This Rexall drugstore, across the street from the Pickwick Block, was owned by different people throughout the years. At the time this photograph was taken, the owner was F.L. "Pop" Hoch, who owned it until 1937. The building continued to operate as a pharmacy until 1968 and closed permanently around 1969.

Here, at the corner of Main and Huntington Streets, the newly constructed Pickwick Block is visible through this arch, which was built in 1937 to help celebrate the formal opening of the Pickwick Theater and the start of the summer season. The arch was removed later that year. The Pickwick Block was envisioned by W.E. Long, who also promoted Syracuse as the "Magnolia City" and planted 200 trees in 1937.

The Pickwick Lounge, located in the Pickwick Block, was an upscale establishment popular with locals and seasonal visitors alike. It opened in 1937. (Courtesy of Garry Ringler.)

Right off the main lounge room was the Alcove Room, showing off the beautiful style of the age. (Courtesy of Garry Ringler.)

The Wawasee Art Gallery, in the Pickwick Block, was operated by Fletcher Marsh Jr. and opened in the early 1940s. Owing to the 1946 Pickwick Block fire, Marsh's artwork is relatively hard to find. Here, a full array of paintings can be seen in the gallery before the fire. (Courtesy of Garry Ringler.)

A theater has existed in downtown Syracuse since the early 1900s. The Theatorium, a wooden structure later renamed the Oakland, burned in 1925. The Pickwick Theater was built in an English Tudor style as part of the Pickwick Block. This classic movie house still features its original Art Moderne–style marquee.

The Pickwick Theater could seat 400, and the English Tudor style prevailed inside as well as outside. (Courtesy of Garry Ringler.)

In 1946, a fire destroyed much of the Pickwick Block. The only building to escape total destruction was the theater, which only lost its lobby and second story. The block was rebuilt in 1947 and destroyed by fire a second time in 1971, when once again the theater survived. It still operates today. The rest of the block was rebuilt with Cape Cod–inspired architecture.

This 1940s view of downtown Syracuse showcases, from left to right, a National Five & Dime Store, the Star Clothing Store, Connolly's Grocery, Pettit's Department Store, and the State Bank Building. Ladies would travel miles to climb the Connolly Building's steep stairway to Louise Connolly's LaPetite Dress Shop, on the second floor (emblazed with "1901" on the front).

This is an 1873 portrait of the students at the Syracuse School, with teacher Hannah Galbreath (seated, center) presiding. In 1906, the owner of this photograph, an E. Kitson, listed the names of each student for a friend—and, unknowingly, for posterity.

This photograph from the very early 1900s shows the staff and students standing in front of the original brick Syracuse School, which was built in 1874.

This 1893 portrait shows the schoolteachers of the Syracuse and Turkey Creek Township schools. J.P. Dolan is seated second from left. Dolan originally came to Syracuse as a timekeeper for the B&O Railroad. He stayed to participate in the founding of almost all of the town's utilities, its educational system, and its library system. He was also a leader in the preservation of local history.

Neighborhood one-room schools with names like Moore, Mock, Darr, Mellinger, Vawter Park, Tamarack, Africa, and Dismal dotted the countryside in Turkey Creek Township. This photograph, taken around 1911, shows students at the Guy school, which taught grades one through eight and still stands on the northeast corner of CR 1000N and Syracuse-Webster Road. Eli Lilly arranged to move the Rothenberger school, a log structure, to Connor Prairie Farm near Indianapolis around 1970. (Courtesy of Garry Ringler.)

"Great Caesar's Ghost!"

This yearbook sketch, made by Syracuse High School student Mary Miles in 1908, apparently depicts a Latin class going awry. The caption reads, "Great Caesar's ghost!"

The junior class at Syracuse High School stands in front of the school in 1911. The man in the back right with the bowler hat is C.C. Bachman, the principal and school superintendent from 1905 to the 1920s, a merchant from 1924 to the 1930s, a member of the first library board, and the 1935 centennial celebration chairman. Descendants of his family have continued to be active in the school system and the community.

This view from South Huntington Street shows the office of the *Syracuse Journal*, the forerunner to the *Mail-Journal* newspaper, whose Syracuse office stands today to the right of the brick hotel on the corner. In the background, both town schools of the time are visible by their peaks. This photograph was taken sometime before 1933, when the school in the upper portion was razed. (Courtesy of Garry Ringler.)

A woodworking class at Syracuse High School works diligently around 1915. The boy holding a hammer in the right foreground is Mel Dillon.

The new Syracuse School, built in 1907–1908, was directly in front of the 1874 school. The first public library in Syracuse was a single room in the basement of this building and opened in 1909. Librarian Ida Knorr was paid an annual salary of $125. Most of the books in the collection were older books from the school's collection. This library was open until 1920. (Courtesy of Chris Harris.)

This photograph shows the cornerstone being laid for the Syracuse School in 1907. During the demolition of the school in 1955, a note written in 1907 by then-student Mary Miles was discovered in the cornerstone. The note was addressed to "the schoolchildren of the future" and read, in part:

> [Though] we may be dead, and our children and our children's children, will not the things we have accomplished, thru each successive generation, make possible things you are to accomplish? In this age of scientific inquiry each generation sees a wonderful advancement over the preceding one. The things that are new and wonderful to us, the telephone, wireless telegraphy, submarines, air-ships, will be to you as a matter-of-course, but these are the gradual outcome of the ages that have gone before as they will be the foundation of what is to follow.

W.A. Jones purchased a milk route from Cal Beck in 1920 and ran the W.A. Jones Dairy, delivering fresh milk to Syracuse-area residents. In 1952, Jones sold his interests to the Crystal Dairy of Warsaw, Indiana, which ended local milk delivery. (Courtesy of Garry Ringler.)

Tired of driving past a dump on the way to his Wawasee home, W.E. Long, a prominent Syracuse booster, promoted an effort around 1933 to clean up this marshy area and turn it into a public park. The town rallied behind the idea, and with help from the Civil Works Administration, a federal job creation program, the former dump became Lakeside Park, which is still a popular park on Syracuse Lake. Warren Colwell is pictured here before the transformation took place.

The Syracuse Public Library, seen here shortly after it was completed in 1921, is one of the few Carnegie library buildings still operating as a library in Indiana. Philanthropist Andrew Carnegie gave a total of $10,000 to Turkey Creek Township to build the freestanding public library. The total cost of construction was between $14,000 and $16,500. The plot of land on which it was built was purchased for $100, and architect S.A. Craig designed the building. While Carnegie allowed any design style to be used, he did make two stipulations: a staircase had to lead up to the front door, symbolizing elevation by learning, and a lamppost had to be installed, to symbolize enlightenment by learning. Although additions have been added to the library since then, both of Carnegie's design stipulations were met and are still present today. (Courtesy of Garry Ringler.)

At one time, Lake Wawasee was home to the smallest post office in the United States. Situated on the Sargent Hotel property, the five-foot-square building had pigeonholes for 30–40 seasonal residents. There was another small post office in Vawter Park. The Wawasee post office closed in the early 1950s.

In the early 1900s, the first rural mail carrier around Lake Wawasee was J.W. "Romey" Deardorff, seen here standing beside his horse-drawn mail cart, pulled by his faithful horse Bird. Mrs. Burlingham, the postmaster for the Buttermilk Point area, stands next to him.

Fred B. Self, another rural mail carrier, had upgraded from a horse-drawn mail cart to an automobile by the time this 1913 photograph was taken. The big smile on his face illustrates his pride. Self served the Syracuse area for 30 years, retiring in 1934.

In 1915, Main Street became the first paved concrete street in Indiana when the local Sandusky Portland Cement Company provided Syracuse with the cement and the town paid the labor costs. McClintic, Colwell & Gordy, a local road building company, paved many streets around town. Note the sign attached to a light pole at lower left advertising "Community Chautauqua."

After the streets in downtown Syracuse were paved, street sweeping was added to the Syracuse town marshal's duties. Here, George Ray, the marshal from 1915 to 1921, sits atop an early street-sweeping wagon, with the sweep brushes attached to the rear.

Two

Hotels and Restaurants

The cool blue waters of Lake Wawasee and Syracuse Lake enticed more than just permanent settlers and fishermen. Situated in an ideal spot close to the thriving cities of South Bend and Fort Wayne and only a few hours from the larger metropolises of Indianapolis and Chicago, city vacationers found a veritable paradise on the shores of the lakes. Beginning in the late 1800s, accessible and affordable rail travel made weekend excursions to the lakes possible for many middle-class city families. At times, wealthier families made it a habit to "summer" at Lake Wawasee, spending weeks in many of the more upscale hotel establishments or building a permanent family vacation cottage on the lakes.

By the early 1900s, many hotels and restaurants catering to people of all economic classes had sprung up around the lakes. The spectacular fishing opportunities, wide-open water for sailing, abundance of shady trees, and sandy beaches meant there was always fun to be had. During the warmer months, the hotels and restaurants in the area played a crucial role in the town's economy, and they also made lasting memories for all who loved their relaxing days on Lake Wawasee and Syracuse Lake.

Several of the hotels that eventually became well known on the lakes started as private residences whose owners would rent out rooms to visitors. As demand rose, homes were expanded and renovated to create proper hotels. Other entrepreneurs, seeing a market for hotels and restaurants, built large establishments that could accommodate hundreds of people at the same time.

Even though a number of the hotels eventually succumbed to fire or financial disaster, their legacy of creating a vacationers' utopia in Syracuse remains to this day.

The Jones Hotel was the first major establishment for entertainment on Lake Wawasee, then known as Turkey Lake. In 1881, Abram and Mary Jones opened a hotel on the north shore near a railroad lean-to station. Abram operated the hotel until 1920, when it was sold. It was eventually converted into a residential home, which was torn down in the early 2000s. (Courtesy of Garry Ringler.)

Klingerman's Store, on Buttermilk Point, operated seasonally for more than 40 years, beginning in the 1890s. Of German-Swiss ancestry, the Klingermans spoke with an accent. Being a large man with a witty personality, Ike Klingerman was a natural at auctioneering. His petite wife, Lavina, raised and educated their family in addition to running the business and renting rooms to fishermen. The site was later developed by the Heil family. (Courtesy of Garry Ringler.)

The land on which the original Vawter Park Hotel was built, seen here before and after the hotel was destroyed by fire in May 1910, had been owned by a series of farmers stretching back to 1846. At the time, the land that became Vawter Park was described as a "dense beech forest" with small creeks feeding into the lake and was mostly uninhabited, according to the 1919 *Standard History of Kosciusko County*. John Terrell Vawter, a banker from Franklin, Indiana, bought the 205-acre property in 1883, built the Vawter Park Hotel on the lakeshore in 1885, and platted the first lake village, Vawter Park, in 1887. The hotel's Victorian decor and friendly, informal atmosphere were its trademarks. In 1907, Vawter sold the hotel to Dr. W.R. McGarvey of Goshen, Indiana. (Above, courtesy of Dave Sheets.)

Following a devastating fire in 1910, the second incarnation of the Vawter Park Hotel was built by Dr. W.R. McGarvey in 1911 on the same site. At that time, accommodations at the hotel were $1.50 a night or $8 a week. The 30-room hotel was described by a contemporary as a comfortable, homelike place.

Another stroke of bad luck hit the hotel a few years later when a kitchen employee turned out to be a carrier of typhoid fever. Between 30 and 50 people died in the resulting epidemic, including Dr. McGarvey's wife. Dr. McGarvey himself passed away in 1916. The hotel was sold to John Boyts before being destroyed by fire again on June 4, 1920. Here, visitors enjoy the veranda a few years before the hotel burned.

From the ashes of the Vawter Park Hotel, Boyts built the South Shore Inn. The inn's sloping lawn facing the lake was a popular spot to sunbathe and watch activities on the water. Boyts sold the hotel to former Indiana state highway commissioner Jap Jones in July 1943. Jones sold the hotel to a syndicate in 1964, and it was destroyed by fire once again in October of that year.

The South Shore Inn was an "American plan" hotel, meaning that food was included in the price of lodging. The Lakefront Lounge, seen here, was a favorite gathering spot for vacationers after a long day playing on and in the lake. (Courtesy of Dave Sheets.)

Oakwood Park, a 40-acre tract of land on the northwest side of Lake Wawasee, was purchased by the Indiana Evangelical Conference in April 1893. Oakwood's first hotel, the Hotel Esther, named after the oldest daughter of Oakwood's superintendent at the time, is seen here in a postcard from 1909. This was the first incarnation of what later became the Oakwood Hotel and then the Oakwood Inn. (Courtesy of Chris Harris.)

The new Oakwood Hotel was built on the site of the Hotel Esther, which was torn down in 1927. The new hotel featured 63 rooms and wraparound screened-in porches facing the lake on both levels. Part of the original pier at Oakwood can also be seen at lower right. (Courtesy of Chris Harris.)

This postcard of the Oakwood Hotel's lobby in 1932 shows it to be simple and comfortable. Note the inverted Latin crosses on the posts; this is known as a Cross of St. Peter or a Petrine Cross.

BATHING SCENE OAKWOOD PARK WAWASEE LAKE IND.

Oakwood Park, with its hills overlooking the lake, winding woods, sports courts, and sandy-bottomed beaches, was and still is a popular destination in Syracuse. The lakefront along Oakwood Park, seen here with swimmers enjoying the water, remains one of the most pristine and scenic stretches of Lake Wawasee. The concrete seawall now present was not built until 1940. (Courtesy of Chris Harris.)

Purchased around 1882 by the Cedar Beach Association, a two-story structure on a cedar-covered bluff on the north shore of Turkey Lake became known as the Cedar Beach Club House. One of the association's most active members was Col. Eli Lilly, founder of the successful pharmaceutical corporation Eli Lilly & Company in Indianapolis. This building with 50 sleeping rooms was primarily a club for wealthy fishing enthusiasts. It burned in the fall of 1891.

Members of the Cedar Beach Club felt they were being confused with Cedar Lake, so Colonel Lilly helped rename both the club and Turkey Lake to Wawasee. In 1892, the Wawasee Inn was built by the Wawasee Club on the site of the former hotel. The inn comprised 30,000 square feet with a dining hall that seated 300. (Courtesy of Chris Harris.)

In an image taken from a 1901 Wawasee Inn advertisement, beautifully dressed ladies pose in a rowboat on the beach in front of the Wawasee Inn. The advertisement also spotlights the nearby mineral springs, which were thought to have medicinal value, a darkroom for guests interested in photography, a livery stable for use by guests, a dance floor, a golf course, a swimming area, and, of course, the inn's seasonal orchestra.

Swimmers enjoy the beach at the Wawasee Inn in the early 1900s. Thanks to the inn's annex, called the Wawasee Villa, and its three large fireplaces, the Wawasee Inn's hotel season ran well into the winter months. However, the greatest foe of any hotel on Wawasee visited the inn within just a few decades after being built—fire burned the hotel to the ground on September 28, 1919.

THE SPINK WAWASEE HOTEL AND COUNTRY CLUB
ON LAKE WAWASEE   WAWASEE, INDIANA

The third time was the charm for the same site that had seen the Cedar Beach Club House and the Wawasee Inn burn. A three-story, pink stucco, 130-room hotel built in the Spanish Revival style was completed in the mid-1920s by the Northern Indiana Hotel Realty Company. The construction contract was awarded to the E.G. Spink Co. of Indianapolis. George Spink was a man so full of ideas that he reportedly had two or three men following him at all times to write down his ideas as they came to him. He promptly named the new hotel the Spink-Wawasee after his family, who also owned the Spink Arms Hotel in downtown Indianapolis. Unfortunately, Spink never lived to see its success; he died less than a year after the hotel opened its doors in 1926.

Many hotels like the Spink would hire a single orchestra to play at the hotel for an entire season, much to the delight of dancers. Here, the Jack Tilson Orchestra, presumably the season's orchestra, sits on the lawn facing Lake Wawasee at the Spink. In later years, Tilson was the first secretary-treasurer of the Wawasee Property Owners Association. (Courtesy of Paul Pollock.)

The Spink was popular with locals as well as with summer visitors. Here, newlyweds James and Patricia Breen (left), along with friends Gene Kalb and Francis Halpin (right), whose families all owned cottages on Wawasee, soak up the sun of a summer day on the Spink's lawn. (Courtesy of the Breen family.)

The Spink was an American plan hotel, and the manager was an Englishman named Arthur Buckley, who insisted on wearing a cutaway coat and bow tie during every shift. He was affectionately known as "Sir Arthur." The hotel's card room was the scene of many enjoyable times.

One of the rooms at the Spink-Wawasee Hotel shows the accommodations to be comfortable and filled with light.

Many personalities of the era, including Abbott and Costello, seen here in 1941 alongside state troopers Bob Clevenger and Sam Patton, stayed at the Spink-Wawasee Hotel. Al Capone's crime syndicate ran the casino in the hotel, which was guarded at all times by two burly bouncers. Syracuse locals rarely stepped foot in the casino. According to colorful local legends, which are most likely untrue, during one of the many gambling raids on the Spink in the 1920s and 1930s, several slot machines, which were then illegal in Indiana, were thrown into the lake by their owners rather than risking being confiscated by law enforcement. Known as the "Monte Carlo of northern Indiana," according to an article dated August 18, 1930, the Spink was often the target of gambling raids. However, the town constables apparently had trouble rounding up enough officers to carry out the raids, as many county officials had been paid off to look the other way on illegal gambling establishments around the lake.

A seaplane lands in front of the Spink in the 1930s, much to the delight of bystanders on shore. Private planes also could land behind the Spink Hotel at the Wawasee Airport, which opened in 1934. (Courtesy of Paul Pollock.)

Unfortunately, the good times did not last. Bonnie Spink Cuniff, dressed in white in the back right, ran the hotel with her husband, Bernard, until 1944, when Bernard passed away. In 1947, Bonnie was traveling through the Smokey Mountains with her sister when a sudden winter storm hit. Sadly, Bonnie died of exposure; shortly thereafter, the hotel was sold to the Crosier Order of the Roman Catholic Church.

Truesdell Lodge, the name given to the collection of rustic log cabins in Brunjes Park, accommodated fishermen and tourists for over 75 years. Mr. Brunjes, an old German man still very much from the old country, ran a small rooming house specializing in German potato salad, fried chicken, and beer. (Courtesy of Garry Ringler.)

Matty Katzer came to the lake in 1908 to help manage the Wawasee Inn. In 1921, he bought the Brunjes Hotel on the southwest shore of Lake Wawasee. The renovated hotel, renamed the Tavern Hotel, quickly became a popular fishing resort. By 1926, the hotel had 35 rooms. What was once a park became a resort known throughout the Midwest.

This Johnson's Hotel pier shows just how far we have come! Early piers were laid on wooden sawhorses. Posts were added later, not to hold the pier but to tie up boats. John Sudlow was a pioneer in the pier business, perfecting the design for interlocking pier sections with half-rounds and plank-type galvanized pier standards. In 1938, Sudlow went into the pier business full time. (Courtesy of Dave Sheets.)

Charles W. Johnson of Indianapolis bought Buttermilk Point from Betty Jarrett's heirs and developed an amusement park complete with a zoo, merry-go-round, excursion boat, and a small hotel on the property. Pictured here at the height of its popularity, Johnson's Hotel boasted a charming dining hall, an annex with sleeping rooms on the water's edge, a sandy beach, and beautiful grounds for guests to explore.

The property was sold in the late-1960s, and the Bay Point condominiums were built in phases on the site. Johnson's Hotel remained in operation a few more years until the contents were sold at auction and the building was razed.

The Lake View Hotel, built by George Lamb, opened in 1898 on what was known as Black Stump Point due to the blackened stumps off its southwestern shore. This area is now known as Waco Point. The rambling, two-story hotel was popular with visitors from the nearby city of Goshen. During the 1907–1908 season, accommodations could be had for $1.50 a night, or $8 a week.

Seen here in July 1911, the Ditton Hotel stood on the south shore of Lake Wawasee. It still exists today as a private home. It was a popular spot with fishermen beginning in the 1890s, and Charles "Billy" Brian, a well-known local sailor and fisherman, may have resided there for many summers. Also known as the Ukumbak, it remained a hotel until the 1930s.

The Crow's Nest started its life as the private residence of early Wawasee settler Nathaniel Crow. After the house was expanded, the Crow's Nest became well known for its comfortable rooms and dining accommodations. A barn on the property also became a summer home for theatrical troupes starting in the 1940s. The Crow's Nest building still stands today. (Courtesy of Dave Sheets.)

J.M. "Jess" Sargent, seen on the far right in his workshop, was one of the best boatbuilders in the area. Sargent originally came to Syracuse around 1899 to work on sailboats for Eli Lilly and others. In 1914, Jess and Laura Sargent started building what would eventually grow to be the three-story Sargent's Hotel beside the pier serving the nearby B&O Railroad depot, the major mode of transportation of the day.

By 1930, Sargent's Hotel had become such a popular destination that multiple additions were built, including broad expanses of porches fronting on the lake. The hotel also sported a sweet shop, a soda fountain, and a bath house where visitors could change into their bathing suits.

With later expansions, the Sargent's Hotel dining rooms could seat 400. The hotel was known for serving delicious "Hoosier-style" meals of prime rib, fried chicken, and roast beef. The food was cooked on a coal-burning stove, and the vegetables were all grown by local farmers. No alcohol was served at the hotel, and the dining rooms were open to both hotel guests and Syracuse locals from April through October.

A staff member mans the cigar stand at Sargent's Hotel. The hotel contents were auctioned off in 1957. The property was sold to the Lilly family, who razed all but one structure, the Porches, which had been built for large parties. The Wawasee Property Owners Association held its pancake breakfasts there for years. In the mid-1970s, this structure was also torn down.

Stretching between the Wawasee Inn, past Sargent's Hotel, and ending at the Jones Hotel was Sunset Lane, also called Lover's Lane, a tree-lined walkway along a scenic section of the lakeshore of Wawasee. Remnants of it can still be found today. (Courtesy of Garry Ringler.)

Built around 1854 by Jacob Renfro on the northeast corner of Main and Huntington Streets, the Lake House Hotel, once called the Fremont House, was an early hotel in Syracuse. It operated until 1896, when it was moved to Front Street in Syracuse. The building still stands today as a private residence, looking much as it does in this picture.

For many years, the Grand Hotel was the only hotel in Syracuse not on one of the lakes. During busy times in the summer, the hotel's restaurant was known to stay open 24 hours a day, which would have been quite a novelty at the time. Although the building still stands in the downtown today, its balconies and signature turret were removed in the 1940s.

Foo and Faye Wong, both natives of China, opened their popular Chinese restaurant in Wawasee Village in 1954 after helping run the Mandarin Inn restaurant and owning the Pagoda Inn restaurant near Wawasee. Foo and Faye's quickly became famous for the enormous handmade eggrolls they made daily. It was not unusual for them to serve 1,000 customers on some holidays, even if it was not during the busy summer season.

The Frog Tavern, a homey little lake restaurant seen here in its earliest incarnation, was started by Charlie Dalke at the west end of Lake Wawasee. In the 1930s, he also owned and operated the Sleepy Owl, on State Road 13 near the south side of the lake. Both eateries were and still are very popular restaurants in the lakes area.

From about 1889 to 1929, the Syracuse post office was in the freestanding building on the south side of Main Street at the western edge of the Syracuse business district. The building, which still stands today, was later used primarily as a restaurant, as seen here, under several different owners. Probably the most well remembered were Pel Clayton's Café and Jim and Dorothy Connolly's Wawasee Restaurant. Later uses included the Syracuse License Branch.

A store owned by Frank Rudy served delicious sundaes in its ice cream parlor. When Louie Solt's grocery opened in the same building, he continued to operate the ice cream parlor, in addition to specializing in fine cuts of meat, fresh fruits, and vegetables. The location, on Lake Wawasee across from the South Shore Inn, was an ideal area for residents as well as travelers. (Courtesy of Garry Ringler.)

The staff at Louie's Grill and Grocery stands ready to serve in the summer of 1940. Specializing in fried chicken, John and Cecelia Solt Sheire were in business for 25 years. It was a thrill for youngsters to go by boat to Louie's for ice cream.

Three

BOATS AND MARINAS

The earliest boats in the area were carved out of tree trunks by Native Americans. Hewn from a single trunk, these dugout canoes were known to the earliest European settlers and explorers as one of the modes of transport on North American waters.

With the coming of the railroad in 1874, hotels were built and passenger steamboats became a common sight on the lakes. To keep steamboats running, a channel was dredged with a loop at its north end, forming an island to circle around near the east side of Pickwick Park to access a coal tipple located along the railroad. Steamboats were often used to pick up passengers arriving by rail and take them to their destinations around the lake: the Jones Hotel and the Wawasee Inn, on the north shore; the log cabin springhouse of Betty "Mother" Jarrett, on the far east shore, to get a cup of buttermilk; the Vawter Park and Lake View hotels, along the south shore; Oakwood Park, on the west shore; and returning to Eppert's Landing, near the old Pickwick railway station, which was abandoned in 1928.

Boats primarily stayed on whichever lake they were launched. At the time, the railroad bridge separating the two lakes was so low that steamships would have to lower their smokestacks in order to pass underneath. Even passengers in rowboats would have to lie in the bottom of their boats in order to get under the bridge. In 1912, the B&O Railroad bridge was raised three feet, enabling easy boat access to both lakes.

As time went on, more sophisticated vessels began to be familiar on Wawasee. Steamboats gave way to passenger launches, which shared the waters with sleek, wooden-hulled speedboats that zipped around the lake. Sailing has always had a serious presence on the lakes, both in the summer and the winter. To accommodate the sailing and boating needs of the lakes, many marinas were established.

The steamboat *Modoc*, seen here in 1875, was the first steamer on Lake Wawasee, which was then still called Nine Mile Lake—and later called Turkey Lake before it became Lake Wawasee. Captained by Frank Reith and with John Egbert as the pilot, the *Modoc* carried passengers, groceries, and mail around the lake.

With the coming of the B&O Railroad in 1874, summer excursions were run to Lake Wawasee. Steamboats plied the waters, transporting passengers to numerous destinations. Abram Jones brought a substantial tug from Chicago by train, launched it off the railroad bridge, and moored it at Jones' landing. After cutting it in two and adding a center section, he named it the Anna Jones after his young daughter. (Courtesy of *Early Wawasee Days*.)

In 1885, John Vawter brought the *Gazelle*, seen here at center left with its flag flying, to Wawasee. It was used primarily for transporting hotel guests to and from the railway depot and as an excursion boat. During the winter, it was removed from the water and stored in a wooden boathouse on the lakeshore near the Vawter home.

Two sailboats cruise by the Eli Lilly estate in 1915. Colonel Lilly began vacationing on Wawasee in the early 1880s, and built the cottage seen here between the sailboats on the north shore in 1887. He instilled his love for sailing in his grandson Eli, who first visited around 1888 and returned every summer until 1976. The house looks much the same today. (Courtesy of Dave Sheets.)

Capt. Edwin C. Rosson's steamer, the *American Girl*, had a steel hull rather than the usual wooden hull. Passenger steamboats often transported guests and their luggage to their destinations for 20¢—10¢ for the passenger and 10¢ for their luggage. On Sundays, the *American Girl* carried vegetables to sell to lake residents.

A group of people pose for a picture next to the *Minnahaha*, a "beautiful and speedy" steam launch, according to an 1896 resident of Pickwick Park. The boat was built in nearby Goshen for George Lamb, the owner of the new Lake View Hotel at Black Stump Point.

The *Wawasee* passenger boat, captained by Captain Rosson, is seen here. In 1912, he launched a locally constructed 40-foot vessel that achieved a top speed of 12 miles per hour with the help of a 5-horsepower gasoline engine. This engine and the recently raised railroad bridge allowed the boat to make a round trip of both lakes in two hours. Rosson was also the caretaker for Pickwick Park.

Steamships docked at the Wawasee Protective Association's pier picked up passengers from the nearby Wawasee depot to ferry them to hotels and cottages. Competition for passengers was fierce. On at least one occasion, a violent fistfight occurred among the captains vying for passengers. Each steamship's whistle was different, meaning that a boat was distinguishable before it could be seen. This picture was taken by a resident of Pickwick Park.

The houseboat *Avalon*, seen above while under construction and below on Wawasee in the early 1900s, was owned by William Fortune, the president of the Indianapolis Telephone Company. Fortune became fascinated with houseboats while traveling the Georgian Bay in Ontario and decided he wanted a floating cottage on Wawasee. Jess Sargent built the houseboat sometime between 1898 and 1902 for a cost of approximately $1,400. It was 66 feet long, 16 feet wide, and slept 12 people. It was towed to the middle of the lake by a small steamer and anchored, but, shortly thereafter, a storm made it heel over dangerously. The next day, it was towed to the southern shore and moored for a few years. It was eventually moved to the northern shore and used as living quarters.

The *Mishler Flyer* is seen here on Lake Wawasee in an undated photograph. In August 1927, the Mishler boat factory, presumed to be in Syracuse, was destroyed by fire.

The *Deluxe* was a gasoline-powered passenger boat operated out of Oakwood Park by the Houston Winters family. Houston "Whit" Winters ran a small grocery and sandwich shop on old State Road 13 between Waco and the Sleepy Owl. The building, now a guesthouse, stands today on Waco Drive. (Courtesy of Chris Harris.)

When the Sandusky Portland Cement Company ceased using the slip to unload marl barges (pictured above), Aldean Strieby and his wife, Irene Macy Strieby, established the Wawasee Slip (seen below) in 1922. It was technically the first true marina on Lake Wawasee. When Aldean passed away shortly thereafter, his wife's brother, Wales Macy, ran the business. Wales and his wife, Grace, owned and operated the Wawasee Slip for many years. Grace continued running it after Wales died in 1980, until she passed away at age 94 in 1996. The Wawasee Slip is still in business today, expertly servicing many of the old "woodies" (wooden-hulled boats) that continue to call the lakes home. Often, one of them can be seen "soaking" in the water on the original hoist. (Courtesy of the Guyas family.)

Jess Sargent built and operated the passenger boat *Falcon*, seen here in an undated photograph at the Sargent's Hotel pier with Sargent himself at the helm. A pleasure cruise around the lake cost 35¢, and Sargent would take his sunset ride whether there were any passengers or not. The boat was operational until 1953. The *Falcon* flag, seen at the front of the boat, is on display at the Syracuse-Wawasee Historical Museum.

Mock's Boat Livery, whose pier is seen here in an undated postcard, was known on Wawasee for renting boats with two-cycle engines that made a distinctive "putt-putt" sound. Dwight and Mabel Mock owned the business. Dwight was a good mechanic and was also known as the go-to man for repairing tires in Syracuse.

This sailboat belonged to Corky Harwood. This undated photograph of it being enjoyed by his daughter captures the joys of sailing the waters of Lake Wawasee.

These sailboats are moored at the Wawasee Yacht Club pier. In 1935, sailors interested in racing their handcrafted Snipe sailboats met on a porch at Bishop's Wawasee Marine Supply Company, on the north shore of the lake. Within three years, the Wawasee Yacht Club hosted the 1938 Snipe Class International Regatta. Upon incorporation in 1939, they bought property just east of the Tavern Hotel, and the club remains very active today.

Sheldon Harkless, seen here in his workshop, constructed the first gasoline and marine engines on the lake. Harkless had worked as a fireman for the B&O Railroad and passed the lakes on his daily route for six years before taking up permanent residence in Syracuse when he was around 22 years old. By age 75, he enjoyed the distinction of being the longest-running businessman in Syracuse.

In 1927, Ken Harkless, Sheldon's son, was building engines for hydroplanes. In the late 1920s, he opened the Wawasee Boat Service with his business partner Lou Seider. By 1937, the Wawasee Boat Company was one of the largest marinas in northeastern Indiana. Harkless ran the company until 1969, and a marina still operates today in the same location.

The Harkless seaplane, emblazoned with the Wawasee Boat Company name, was often seen around the lake. Here, in a promotional shot, Ken Harkless fishes off his plane, with the Spink-Wawasee Hotel in the far left background.

Harry McClintic built this motorized iceboat, seen here on Syracuse Lake in 1919.

People on the lakes have always loved boat races, whether they are held on water or on ice. Here, a large group of people prepares for an iceboat race on Syracuse Lake in the 1930s.

This photograph from around 1920 shows the *Miss Detroit II* being readied for a ride on Wawasee by new owner Ralph Teetor (left), accompanied by Lothair Teetor (on bow) and an unidentified driver. When the boat won the Gold Cup Race in Minneapolis in 1917, it was driven by Gar Wood, the famous motorboat builder and water speed world record holder. The original engine was destroyed during a 1918 race.

Larry Griffith purchased the Ross Greenwalt Boat Livery, on the southeast bay of Lake Wawasee, in 1946. In this aerial view from around 1947, the "kettle" between the marina and Morrison Island is well defined. Griffith's Wawasee Marina continues to be owned and operated by the family today. Griffith helped organize the first Wawasee Flotilla in 1961, drove the lead boat for the event for many years, and served as its commodore in 1978.

Ideal Beach Sales and Service was established by Jack and Dorothy Vanderford in 1946. They sold and serviced Martin and then Johnson motors, rented rowboats, sold gas, and carried fishing tackle and snacks in their store. As one of the first Starcraft boat dealers, the next year's models were brought from the nearby factory in Goshen to be tested and photographed on Lake Wawasee, as seen here. (Courtesy of Ann Vanderford Garceau.)

During the busiest days of Waco and the hotels on Lake Wawasee in the 1930s and 1940s, there were several handsome wooden-hulled speedboats used to transport passengers in style to and from their destinations. The *Zip*, *Miss Waco*, and *Miss Miami* seem to wait patiently for the fun to begin in this 1930s photograph.

Providing a smooth ride even when fully loaded with passengers, the 28-foot Gar Wood boat known as the *Blue Streak* was operated out of Bishop's Wawasee Marine Supply Company. It was well known to locals and vacationers alike on Lake Wawasee. Here, the *Blue Streak* is seen in front of the Spink-Wawasee Hotel.

The *Flash II*, another speedy passenger boat in the 1930s, is seen here in front of the Wawasee Boat Service. The Hackercraft had previously belonged to the Noll family before becoming the flagship of Bishop's Wawasee Marine Supply Company.

From left to right, John Rinker, Stover Hire, Bud Hursh, and Jim and Jan Rinker return victorious from racing their stock runabouts in Wisconsin. Hire went on to win numerous national championships in B-stock runabouts and was voted into the Gulf Racing Hall of Fame in the mid-1960s. From these humble beginnings, the Rinker Boat Company is now the oldest American boat brand in continuous production. (Courtesy of Lera Reinholt.)

Four

NEIGHBORHOODS AND ISLANDS

The neighborhoods and islands that comprise Syracuse and Lake Wawasee are the heart and soul of the area. Many neighborhoods, roads, and streets were named after their first permanent settlers. Land development was an important component of making the area around the lakes desirable and livable. Some areas were swampy, while others were quite low and sandy or perched near slow-moving water that would cause mosquitoes to fester. Often, developing land required dredging parts of the shore, or filling in low spots to create lots. Building and moving existing roads as more cottages began to be built was also an important part of the development process, eventually making all areas of the lake accessible.

With each generation giving way to a new one, stories and personages passed into history. The time of the Native Americans riding their horses across the sandbar to Ogden Island passed into the time of settlers in log cabins on the shoreline; this too passed as new houses were built, new citizens were born, and the town of Syracuse formed a cohesive identity. Central to this identity were the neighborhoods where these stories played out and the people who made them special places to live.

Boaters enjoy cool buttermilk and other refreshments at Buttermilk Point on the southeastern shore of Lake Wawasee. Run by the Jarrett family, steamboats often stopped there on their journey around the lake. The small cabin would be crowded with visitors enjoying sweet milk, ice cream, and buttermilk courtesy of the usually barefoot Betty "Mother" Jarrett, who was assisted by her blonde-haired daughter Goldie Alice.

When settlers first began settling on what was known as Eagle Island, on the east side of Lake Wawasee, they found bald eagles nesting annually. The Morrison family was the first generation of permanent settlers on the island, which was later called Morrison Island. Before a bridge was built to the island, between 1907 and 1911, people would ford the water to reach the island. (Courtesy of Dave Sheets.)

In 1929, John Dillinger, arriving under the name "Mr. Smith," allegedly rented a cottage on Morrison Island for a short time before his death in Chicago. Later, when the landlord saw a picture of Dillinger in the newspaper, he was shocked to find Mr. Smith's true identity. During Dillinger's stay, neighbors were reportedly too scared to report him to the police. (Courtesy of Dave Sheets.)

The original name for the area that was eventually called Natti Crow Beach was Sheep Wash, derived from the custom of farmers running their sheep through the waters of the flat beach to wash their coats before shearing. It was homesteaded in 1848 by pioneer Nathaniel Crow. By the time of Crow's death in 1912, the family had accumulated between 500 and 600 acres of local land. (Courtesy of Chris Harris.)

Cedar Point shows evidence of being the oldest site of human habitation on the lake. Parts of the hill were leveled over the years as fill for the lower ground. Here, campers seine for fish in 1910. (Courtesy of Dave Sheets.)

A 1903 map showed Ogden Island as completely surrounded by water and swamp. Eventually, the swampy areas were filled with gravel and sand, stretching from the high ground of Nordyke Park to Ogden Island itself, making it a peninsula, as can be seen in this later aerial view of the area. (Courtesy of Chris Harris.)

The Church of the Little Flower, a Catholic church near the Spink-Wawasee Hotel, was dedicated July 25, 1926. Being located on the water's edge, parishioners could boat to worship. The building was used as a Catholic church until 1965, when it was converted into a dormitory for the Wawasee Preparatory School. The building is now a retreat used by the Fort Wayne and South Bend Diocese of the Catholic Church.

The Rockwell Gift Shop, between the Lilly home and Sargent's Hotel, was operated by the Rockwell sisters of Goshen. The original location was in Nordyke Park, but Mrs. J.K. Lilly Sr. enjoyed frequenting the shop so much that it was relocated to this white Colonial house on the Lilly property. (Courtesy of Dave Sheets and Garry Ringler.)

The Wright's Place neighborhood was platted by Commodore John F. Wright, a physician from Columbus, in the late 1890s. Wright was a founder of the first Wawasee Yacht Club. William A. Hoops, a Goshen native and a successful importer and wholesaler in Chicago, bought lots from Commodore Wright. Soon after, he built this house, naming it Linger Lodge. Today his descendants still enjoy the home, portions of which are virtually unchanged. (Courtesy of Debbie Smith.)

Jones' Landing is seen here on a postcard dated September 1916. The landing was the home of the Jones Hotel. (Courtesy of Dave Sheets.)

During the early days of settlement, Willow Grove was called Conrad's Island after Henry Conrad, who would return to camp alone in a shack each year until he was almost a centenarian. Here, a man fishes in the beautiful waters to the west of Willow Grove in Gordinier Marsh, the marshy area around the inlet to what is now the Wawasee Boat Company, on the northern end of Lake Wawasee.

William Dillon, described by contemporaries as a reclusive fisherman and nature-lover, was an early settler in the 1860s of what became Pickwick Park, the channels of which are seen here before the area was developed. He was killed in the late 1800s while trying to cross one of the two expansive B&O Railroad trestles that bridged the marshy area between the two lakes.

George Lamb and Joseph Moore were early developers of Pickwick Park on Kale Island. The Milford Clubhouse and several other cottages were built in Pickwick Park in the 1890s. Eventually, residents of the neighborhood became co-owners of the land in the park, which had its own caretaker. (Courtesy of Dave Sheets.)

The Game Lodge, pictured here on W.E. "Ed" Long's Bonnie Brae estate, was built to entertain guests. The estate also included a main house and a guesthouse on the lake, spectacular gardens, and, as the sales brochure stated, an "exotically beautiful" Chinese house on Dream Island. Ed Long was a pioneer in the baking industry in Chicago.

J.P. Dolan developed land on Kale Island, which was named after Kale Oram, who settled there in the late 1850s. Land modifications like those pictured here sculpted the landscape to make way for housing developments. Originally a kind of sporting camp for avid fisherman, Kale Island's housing industry began to boom in the late 1920s. The handwriting on this image reads, "Lots for sale – Easy Terms."

Small neighborhood grocery stores, like King's Grocery, seen here on Kale Island, served neighborhoods around the lake. In an era of one-car families, the wife and children might be left without transportation during the week, so these grocery stores became gathering places. As few cottages had telephones, King's employees would summon people to their phone if someone called for them. (Courtesy of Garry Ringler.)

Onkwood Park. Lake Wawasee.

In 1892, the Indiana Evangelical Conference became interested in purchasing the land that eventually became Oakwood. A church report noted that the land had historically been used by "a class of people who imbibed intoxicants frequently with consequent behavior." They purchased the land in 1893 at a price of $5,000. Seen here is the main road through Oakwood. Several of these cottages still stand today. (Courtesy of Chris Harris.)

Imagined as a center for spiritual life, the auditorium, the interior of which is seen here, was remodeled in 1936 and was sometimes used by other groups because of the building's then-modern amenities. (Courtesy of Chris Harris.)

A couple driving through Oakwood Park enjoys the views from their early Buick, made between 1908 and 1910, around the time this picture was taken. They are driving through what became known to Oakwood residents as the orchard, which looks much the same today as it does here. The road also still exists, although it was paved in 1941.

John Stetler of the B&O Railroad bought lot No. 34 in Oakwood and built Oak Park Villa (cottage on right) around 1896. In 2000, a campaign by the Friends of Pioneer Cottage, as Oak Park Villa came to be called, led to the restoration of the cottage to preserve early Oakwood history and provide a summer rental home for families. The committee raised $125,000, well over its original $50,000 goal. Restoration work was completed in August 2001. (Courtesy of Chris Harris.)

When the area first began to be settled, Conkling Bay was comprised of a small but deep portion of open water fringed with shallow marshes. It was a popular fishing spot. The marshes receded as boat traffic increased, and houses were built overlooking Conkling Bay, including the cottages in this photograph. The white cottage on the right belonged to the Baughman family of Goshen and Chicago. (Courtesy of the Breen family.)

South Park, located on the southern shore of Lake Wawasee, was developed in the 1890s by Charles A. Sudlow and Maj. Fletcher E. Marsh. Being a lover of nature, Major Marsh surrounded his home, called The Oaks, with flowers in continuous bloom, fruits in all seasons, and trees that provided a mass of beautiful foliage. Visitors could often find him outside in his gardens. (Courtesy of Dave Sheets.)

If one belonged to the Travelers Protective Association (TPA), they could use the TPA clubhouse on Ideal Beach, which featured individual bedrooms and common living areas in a comfortable dormitory style. Several people from Wabash owned cottages in the Ideal Beach area as a result of becoming acquainted with the lake through the TPA clubhouse. (Courtesy of Dave Sheets.)

Around 1921, Jake Kreig of Wabash built a large wooden toboggan slide as the main attraction of the Ideal Beach amusement area, which also had miniature golf and a sandwich shop on the south shore of Lake Wawasee. Across State Road 13, tourists could stay in cabins or rent rooms at Ideal Lodge. A baseball diamond, picnic shelter, and campgrounds were also available. It remained active through the early 1940s.

This Ideal Beach cottage was built in 1916 by Marcus and Minnie White of Noblesville, Indiana. As was typical of the day, a pitcher pump supplied water, as there was no inside plumbing. An apartment over the garage provided a living area for domestic help. Improvements were made over the generations as their descendants continue to enjoy Lake Wawasee today, but the original look of the cottage is still quite evident. (Courtesy of Helen White Yoder.)

Built around 1905 by Rudolph and Eugenie Desjardins of Chicago, this home and various outbuildings cost $8,000 to construct. It was lit by carbide gas before electricity became available. A windmill pumped water into the home. After Eugenie's death in 1909, Rudolph exchanged the house for property in Chicago. Located on State Road 13, the house has been a bed-and-breakfast for many years.

HONEYWELL COTTAGE

This south shore home was built by Wabash resident Mark Honeywell, the developer of a water heating system that grew into the well-known Honeywell Inc., manufacturers of thermostats and automatic controls for heating systems. The bar in the home's basement was surrounded by a lighted, hand-painted mural of the Miami skyline, to give one the feeling of standing on the afterdeck of Honeywell's yacht in Biscayne Bay watching the sunset. (Courtesy of Dave Sheets.)

This road, with the Vawter Park Hotel visible at the end of the street, was built sometime in the late 1880s. Later, it became the original State Road 13, which followed the southern and western shorelines of Lake Wawasee.

The 1895 report of the Indiana University biological station mentions using a reception room at the Pottawatomie Club, seen here, in Vawter Park. The pier was sizeable enough for steamers to dock, pick up, and deliver passengers. The building, also known as Lookout Cottage since it was first built very near the shoreline, was moved back at a later date. (Courtesy of Dave Sheets.)

This photograph of the All Saints Episcopal Church in Vawter Park was taken in 1908. Just a year earlier, the church had been built and consecrated by Bishop White, Charles Sudlow, and Col. Eli Lilly. The church was used only as a summer chapel until 1966, when a retreat and conference center was added to the grounds. This original church was razed in 1999 and a new church constructed. (Courtesy of Dave Sheets.)

In 1898, Trinity Evangelical Church, seen here on Harrison Street, and Lakeside United Brethren Church, on Lake Street, were built in Syracuse. The Trinity Ladies Aid Society kept active in 1906, holding ice cream socials and selling aprons and sunbonnets. In 1916, Laura Kline pastored the Lakeside church even before women had the right to vote. The two churches merged in 1951, and Trinity is now condominiums.

A 1900 group portrait shows members of the Syracuse Methodist Church congregation, which had a presence in the community as early as 1869. The cornerstone of the church was laid in June 1886.

Grace Evangelical Lutheran Church was formally organized in 1885, and its church building was constructed on East Main Street in Syracuse in the early 1900s. The interior is seen here. The original sanctuary is still used today, but the structure has been remodeled and enlarged.

This 1911 photograph of residential Main Street looks toward the railroad tracks, with the neighborhood sporting sidewalks made of wooden slats, which predated the now-customary concrete sidewalks.

This 1886 view of East Main Street overlooks the southeastern portion of Syracuse and Syracuse Lake. Built in 1850, the white building at center is one of the earliest structures in Syracuse. At one time, it housed a gas station and then a print shop. After renovations drastically altered its appearance, the building was returned to its original exterior condition and remains in active commercial use today.

The home of Sol Miller, president of the Syracuse Bank, is seen here under construction. Responding to a call in 1933 that the "bank examiner's" car had broken down north of town, Miller arrived to help, only to be bound, gagged, and tied to a tree by two men intent on robbing Miller's bank. Before Miller could be freed, the men did indeed rob the Syracuse Bank and escaped using Miller's car.

This photograph shows the Syracuse Church of God, built in 1866 on East Washington Street. Syracuse Lake appears in the background. By 1883, four different denominations were holding services in the building. Today, it is the oldest continually operating church in Syracuse, although the building has undergone extensive renovations inside and out.

The Blanchard home, on the corner of the Syracuse-Webster Road and East 1200 North, known locally as "Crazy Corners," is still standing, looking much the way it does in this early photograph. In 1869, Mr. H. Blanchard was the hostelry manager for the Lake House Hotel.

Five

PASTIMES, CELEBRATIONS, AND SERVICE

Celebrations and fun are important for any community, but doubly so for a community that is so well loved by seasonal visitors and tourists who return year after year to enjoy their favorite activities. Visitors and locals alike have enjoyed golf courses, parks, band concerts, fireworks, sailing races, street fairs, and boat parades. Hotels and other amusement areas sported water slides, toboggan rides, small zoos, sandy-bottomed beaches, and diving platforms.

Fraternal, civic, and social clubs in Syracuse, far too numerous to comprehensively cover in a single chapter, were also a crucial part of community life. Their contributions to improving the area have been invaluable. School activities such as athletics, plays, and musical groups gave students a chance to explore their talents and share them with the community. Basketball was an especially important sport in Syracuse schools, and organized basketball teams in Syracuse have existed for over 100 years.

Live music, played by both local and touring bands, was enjoyed by people of all walks of life. Syracuse was a musical community, with weekly band concerts in the downtown square and local cornet bands and nationally renowned bands playing at local places like the Waco Dance Hall. Parades to celebrate various milestones and holidays were, and continue to be, a gesture of community spirit.

Retiring in his thirties after having sold his electrical company, later called Delco-Remy, Frank Remy built the Wawasee Golf Club behind the Wawasee Inn in 1913. He frequently boated across the lake to work from his Vawter Park home. Many local boys became caddies for the princely wage of 10¢ an hour during the Depression. In 2000, the course was revamped to nine holes. (Courtesy of Dave Sheets.)

For many, playing a round of miniature golf is a summer tradition. The North Shore Miniature Golf Course, behind the Sargent's Hotel, is seen here. In 1930, W.T. Rice developed 18 challenging holes of miniature golf in the Turtle Bay area, along old State Road 13. Across from the Oakwood entrance, Rue Hunnicutt also had a course in his amusement park in the 1940s and 1950s.

In 1924, the South Shore Golf Course began to be developed by Dick Tuttle and his son Carl, who partnered with landowner Roy Brown. Much of the work on the 125-acre property was done by horse-drawn equipment. Pine trees planted along State Road 13 survive today. The actual formal opening in 1932 brought former PGA touring professional Tommy Armour to play the course. (Courtesy of Dave Sheets.)

A golf course with rolling fairways near Syracuse Lake was designed in the mid-1920s by William B. Langford, a friend of noted golf course designer Trent Jones. The distinctive terrain of what became Maxwelton Golf Course was created using mules. Here, the course superintendent's dog Max is pictured on the 18th green with the clubhouse in the background. (Courtesy of the Carlson family.)

Tennis is a popular summer sport around the lakes. In this postcard, guests at the Wawasee Inn play on the hotel's court in the 1910s. (Courtesy of Chris Harris.)

Baseball was another popular sport in Syracuse. This early Syracuse team poses in their uniforms. The Syracuse Grays, an independent baseball team, played other area teams in the 1920s and 1930s. Court Slabaugh was the manager.

A Syracuse baseball team lounges between games in this informal portrait. Only a few of the members have been identified: in the third row, Dick Miller stands third from the left, Wes Hire is fourth from the left, and Emery Strieby is second from the right. In the second row, Roscoe Howard is second from the right.

The 1919 Syracuse High School basketball team was coached by Cal Beck, a well-known farmer and educator in Syracuse who started his teaching career in small country schools. He was the Turkey Creek Township trustee in the 1950s, and also developed a residential area on the east side of Bonar Lake, dredging, filling, and selling lots. Freshman Emery Druckamiller scored 32 points in the sectionals to become the tournament's most valuable player.

The 1920s were the Emery Druckamiller years in Syracuse. This 1920–1921 Syracuse High School basketball team, led by coach Court Slabaugh and all-state player Druckamiller, went as far as the Sweet 16, only to lose to Huntington 20-16, with Druckamiller scoring all 16 points. After a successful athletic career at Indiana University, Druckamiller returned to Syracuse in 1926 to coach the team to a sectional title.

The members of the 1936 Kosciusko County Championship team were, from left to right, (first row) James Miller, Ezra Halsey, Howard Juday, Harold Kline, Nelson Auer, Robert Hinderer, Ernest Strock, Oliver Hibschman, and Burton Niles; (second row) Coach Clare Holly, Ed Coy, James Stucky, George Bill Smith, Dewitt Disher, Herschel Bitner, Earl Held, Herman Doll, Richard Beck, and manager Bert Ward.

After winning the 1949 sectionals at Warsaw, this Syracuse High School basketball team had the thrill of playing in the regionals at Fort Wayne North Side, the home court of the Zollner Pistons. The team included, from left to right, (first row) John Kroh, Jack Darr, Bud Dietrick, Lowell Barnhart, and Gary Meek; (second row) Bob Hoover, Brent Bushong, Jake Bitner, Roger Fry, Gene Kitson, and coach Millard Sink. (Courtesy of Jack Darr.)

The ice hockey team at Wawasee Preparatory School, which was then in the former Spink-Wawasee Hotel, practices on the frozen surface of the lake in the 1960s.

The Syracuse High School band is seen here in 1949, with twirlers (from left to right) Barbara Bowser, Mary Janette Payser, and Sasha Hire standing in the front. After high school graduation, Bowser and Cynthia Frevert performed in the Ringling Bros. circus for a time in the 1950s, and Sasha Hire was a music major at Indiana University.

This 1938 portrait of the Syracuse High School band conducted by Willard Gustafson shows what a large ensemble it was. The trombone player with dark hair seated in front of the tuba is Ron Sharp, who was later a journalist, Syracuse town historian, and the designated Kosciusko County historian.

Wawasee Post No. 223 of the American Legion was organized in 1933. The Legion's Drum and Bugle Corps, seen here in 1941 in front of the Syracuse High School, featured majorette Sasha Hire (center) who always charmed the crowd during parades. The 1955 Drum and Bugle Corps won first place in Class B competition in Indianapolis under the direction of Millard "Cy" Hire.

In May 1935, the "Biggest Affair Ever Staged in Syracuse," according to the playbill, was a humorous play called *Womanless Wedding*, sponsored by the Men's Brotherhood of the Methodist Episcopal Church and performed by a 60-member, all-male cast in the Syracuse High School auditorium. The play was a satire about weddings, and tickets cost 15¢. A $50 donation from the proceeds was given to the Methodist Episcopal Ladies Aid.

IF YOU WANT TO LAUGH—COME TO THE

"Womanless Wedding"
to be presented at
SYRACUSE HIGH SCHOOL AUDITORIUM
By SYMPSON-LEVIE COMPANY, of Bardstown, Kentucky.
SPONSORED BY MENS BROTHERHOOD OF M. E. CHURCH

60 --- Local Men as Characters --- 60
SCREAMS OF LAUGHTER!   BE SURE TO COME!
BIGGEST AFFAIR EVER STAGED IN SYRACUSE, INDIANA

All Star Cast Headed with LLOYD DISHER as Leading Lady

Butler .... John Harley
Punch Girls .... Don Perry
           Junior Jones
Present Girls ...... Ross Anderson
           Ralph Thornburg, Jr.
Bride's Weeping Mother
           John Grieger
Bride's Comforting Father
           Nelson Miles
Bride's Bad Little Brothers
   E. O. Dunn and Haltie Holloway
Old Maid Aunt ..... W. O. Connolly
Bride's Grandmother
           John McGarrity
Bride's Grandfather - F. W. Greene
Charlie Chaplin ... Franklin Rhode
Uncle of Groom from Milford
   Junction .... Fred Self
Aunt of Groom from Milford
   Junction .... A. A. Pfingst
Mae West .... Carl Tuttle
Twin Sisters of the Bride
   Clarence Snyder, Chester Workman
Mary Pickford ... Merritt Richhart
Sis Hopkins ...... Everett Fetters
Groom's Haughty Mother
           Melburn Rapp
Groom's Haughty Father
           Noble Blocker
The Fashion Plate ...... Bill Smith
Sir Harry Lauder . Emeral Callender
Kentucky Colonel ..... D. L. Gibson
Kentucky Lady .... Ray Foster
Country Cousin ...... Barney Davis
Bing Crosby .... Victor Sawallash
Long Lost Brother of the Bride
           Harry Porter
President Roosevelt ... W. C. Gants

Mrs. Roosevelt .... R. E. Blue
Pat O'Grady .... Pell Clayton
Rosie O'Grady ..... Ernest Richards
Henpecked Husband
           Vernon Beckman
Devoted Wife ..... Bert Whitehead
Annie Laurie . Rev. J. S. Pritchard
Negro Mammy ...... Orbra Bobeck
Baby Sister .... James Butt
Rastus .... Orval Snobarger
Sambo .... Paul Bushong
Madame Galli Curci . Walter Smith
Village School Marm
           Dr. Garnett Latham
Vamp from Hollywood
           Robert Strieby
Lawrence Tibbett .. Mark Schrock
           BRIDAL PARTY
Bishop .... Burton Howe
Best Man ..... Travis Purdy
Groom's Men .... A. E. Miller
           G. R. Johnson
           Richard Isbell
           James Stockey
Bride's Maids .... Chester Langston
           Ross Anderson
           Burris Sharp
Matron of Honor .... Harry Culler
Maid of Honor ..... Roy Schlester
Flower Girls .... A. W. Geyer
           R. W. Osborn
Bride .... Lloyd Disher
Groom .... GUESS WHO? ? ?
Train Bearer ...... A. W. Emerson
Ring Bearer .... Dave Brown
Accompanist .... Ned Harley
Director ...Miss Edith Mary Woodard

Thursday and Friday, May 16 - 17, 1935

Cornet bands with all-brass instruments traditionally played fanfares and other types of traditional American music in the mid-to-late 1800s. Here, the Syracuse Silver Cornet Band poses with their instruments in this 1895 portrait. In 1920, the newspaper reported that the Medusa Cornet Band played on the town square each Wednesday evening during the summer, with C.C. Bachman directing.

In 1935, Syracuse celebrated its 100th birthday with a large parade. Here, marching bands and decorated vehicles make their way down Main Street as crowds watch.

J.P. Dolan arranged for the first Decoration Day commemoration in May 1877. The tradition continues today, with a parade down Main Street to the Syracuse Cemetery to honor veterans. Seen here leading the parade on Memorial Day 1937 are, from left to right, Tom Felts, Harry Cleveland, Roscoe Howard, and Jim Searfoss. Joe Hughes, age nine, joins them at far right. Cy Hire leads the drum and bugle corps. (Courtesy of Garry Ringler.)

Civil War veterans of the Syracuse area–based Lakeview Post No. 246 of the Grand Army of the Republic, organized in 1879, reunite in front of the building on the southwest corner of West Main Street and Huntington Street (State Road 13). The Veterans Memorial in Crosson Park honors Syracuse residents who served their country in war.

113

The Syracuse Home Guard stands in formation at the intersection of Main Street and Huntington Street (State Road 13) on Armistice Day, November 11, 1918. Not surprisingly, most of the soldiers are smiling. The Grand Hotel, Syracuse Power & Light, and the Sloan Restaurant stand behind them. Note the gentleman on the far left sitting on a horse dressed as Uncle Sam, complete with a flag-themed stovepipe hat.

Chicago businessman W.E. Long's Dream Island was an Oriental garden featuring a teahouse built on pilings between two small islands connected by an arched bridge, with exotic birds and equally exotic lotus flowers (which were promptly eaten by local beavers). When Long first came to Syracuse in 1923, the swampy area behind Kale Island was uninhabited.

W.E. Long (right) stands inside the teahouse explaining a rare piece of Chinese art to Greta Florey (center) and Laura Jane Deady (left) prior to the opening of his Chinese museum on September 4, 1936. His Chinese art collection was the only one of its kind in Indiana at that time. The setting practically duplicated a wooded island in Chicago's Jackson Park. (Courtesy of Garry Ringler.)

Fred Hinderer, dressed for flying, waits for an airplane in a field between the railroad tracks and Chicago Street in Syracuse. This picture was taken in 1915, when flying would have still been a novelty. Hinderer was a manager of the Kelly House, the town's second hotel, which opened in 1879 in a rambling two-story frame house on the southeast corner of Washington and Huntington Streets.

Will Tucker spent his summers on Wawasee in the 1890s at the Cedar Beach Club, and later at a cottage just to the east. Known as a talented and charismatic musician, Tucker composed "Wawasee Waltz" in 1894. He and his brother Charles were also skillful sailors, winning the Wawasee Yacht and Canoe Club Cup in 1890 and 1895. Unfortunately, both of them died as young men.

The original Waco, which stood for Wawasee Amusement Company, opened in 1915. It was smaller than the later building and was originally planned as a floating dance hall. Featuring afternoon and evening dancing along with moving pictures and light refreshments, its popularity grew, and by the 1920s, building expansions had created a large covered pavilion space. Here, the band and employees enjoy the view on Waco's pier in August 1915.

Countless top bands, including Glenn Miller and Benny Goodman, played at Waco during its heyday. Cab Calloway drew an estimated crowd of 4,000 in the 1930s, and Glenn Miller attracted between 7,000 and 10,000 in 1941. During the day, the public could swim, go for speedboat rides, and enjoy the water slide. Here, Jack Vanderford drives the *Zip* fully loaded with passengers. (Courtesy of Garry Ringler.)

Virginia Hay, an area resident at the time, recalled in *Kosciusko County: An Oral and Pictorial History*, "When the big bands appeared, the crowds were so large that dancing was impossible. In those cases, people simply stood, listened and watched the musicians. Waco had a dance floor that was polished until it glimmered like moonlight." Waco's dance floor is seen here during its height. Waco was torn down in 1957. (Courtesy of Dave Sheets.)

Pickwick Bowling Lanes, seen here, was located in the basement of the Pickwick Block. (Courtesy of Garry Ringler.)

Thrill-seekers loved the toboggan slide at Ideal Beach. Racing down the slide, the sled would skim over the surface of Wawasee for quite a distance before sinking into the cool waters. The slide's klaxon horn, which was blown when a sled was let loose, could be heard clear across the lake. Many delightful times were enjoyed there until World War II brought gas rationing, cutting back recreational travel. (Courtesy of Dave Sheets.)

118

Swimming and playing in the water are fun activities for everyone on the lake. Here, a group of boys create a pyramid in front of the Spink-Wawasee Hotel.

Clubs have also been a part of the social life of Syracuse residents since the time of the first settlers. Here, the Syracuse Art Club donates a painting to the Syracuse Public Library. This painting still hangs proudly in the library today.

The Syracuse Fraternal Order of Eagles and their guests are seen here during its first annual banquet in May 1908.

For several years, weekly band concerts performed on a raised platform at the corner of Main and Huntington Streets were a tradition in Syracuse during the warmer months. This band performs in front of the Grand Hotel while a large crowd watches.

The Smith Walbridge Camp was founded on Bonar Lake as a baton-twirling school in 1949. Eventually, its offerings grew to include programs for majorettes, drill teams, color guards, cheerleaders, and marching bands. Over 5,000 students attended each summer, many coming by train. In 1990, the campgrounds were sold and the programs were moved to the University of Illinois and then to Eastern Illinois University. The clinics continue to be successful. (Courtesy of Chris Harris.)

"When will the car go through the ice?" was a lighthearted fundraiser held during winter in which a car would be placed on the frozen lake and guesses were made about when it would finally break through the ice. Here, the car from the previous winter is pulled out of Syracuse Lake in 1960.

Ice fishing has always been a popular wintertime sport on the lakes. The channels and bays of the lakes were especially popular spots for ice fishermen.

Charlie Dalke is seen here with his mobile food cart on the frozen surface of Lake Wawasee. Both Dalke and his cart are wearing skates. Dalke would fill his cart with hot coffee and sandwiches and then travel out to the ice fishermen to sell his goods. Dalke went on to establish both the Frog Tavern and the Sleepy Owl Restaurant.

122

The boating fun did not end in the wintertime, as iceboats were popular on the lakes. The lightweight crafts were designed to harness the wind in their sails, propelling them on wooden runners secured underneath the seating area. Here, a group from Perfect Circle Piston Ring Corp. gathers in front of the Dan Teetor home on Lake Wawasee around 1939 and poses on an iceboat.

A fishing trip was bound to be successful if led by Marion Morrison of Morrison Island, one of the lake's best fishing guides, who stands proudly with the day's catch in this early photograph. (Courtesy of *Early Wawasee Days*.)

This massive sturgeon was retrieved from the water near Vawter Park in 1910 by Charlie Dalke, who stands beside it. The man with the hat is Julius Reiss of New York City, who was in the area to visit his daughter Adeline Reiss Sudlow (Mrs. Arthur). Sturgeon have been the source of many lake tales, including one caught by Dave Riddle in 1991 that was immortalized in a ballad.

Pike, perch, bluegills, and crappies are some of the most sought-after fish in area lakes. Here, it appears as though the Sargent's Hotel cooks are about to have a bountiful fish fry. Fishing guides made their living taking visiting fishermen to their favorite fishing holes. Some older residents recalled watching fishermen walk by with a large pike slung over their shoulder.

Bicycling was a popular mode of transportation in the early 1900s. Here, Hester Rosenberger, sister of Mrs. Sheldon Harkless, poses proudly next to her bicycle with Syracuse Lake in the background.

Jubilee Days were sponsored by the Syracuse Commercial Club as a homecoming celebration. A balloon ascension held during the September 1909 event proved exciting to Syracuse resident Quinter Neff. The young man was helping with ropes when suddenly he found himself ascending with the balloon, with the rope wrapped around him. Fortunately, Quinter and the balloon landed safely at the Kern farm, a half mile from town.

MAIN ST., LOOKING EAST, SYRACUSE, IND.

Sitting by the lake and enjoying the view is a popular activity regardless of the era, as evidenced by this serene scene of three people relaxing on a swing at the Wawasee Inn. They may just be fortunate enough to catch a glimpse of "golden windows," created by the reflection of the rising or setting sun on houses across the lake. (Courtesy of Dave Sheets.)

This early automobile, seen on the shore of Syracuse Lake with Sheldon Harkless at the wheel, was manufactured in the Harkless machine shop on the lake in 1905. The Mier Carriage Company of nearby Ligonier produced between 10 and 20 of these vehicles during a two-year period. A Mier car is now the centerpiece of the Syracuse-Wawasee Historical Museum.

BIBLIOGRAPHY

Coplen, Daniel L. *Kosciusko County: An Oral and Pictorial History.* Warsaw, IN: Kosciusko County Historical Society, 1997.

Edgell, Scott A. *Sketches of Lake Wawasee.* Indianapolis, IN: Indiana Historical Society, 1967.

Laughner, Julie Clifton. *The People of Pickwick Park.* Indianapolis, IN: CreateSpace Independent Publishing Platform, 2013.

Lilly, Eli. *Early Wawasee Days.* Indianapolis, IN: The Studio Press, 1965.

Madison, James H. *Eli Lilly: A Life, 1885–1977.* Indianapolis, IN: Indiana Historical Society, 1989.

Maidenburg, Meyer. *Short History of Morrison Island.* 1979.

Miles, George William and Preston. *Biennial Report of the Commissioner of Fisheries and Game of Indiana.* Indianapolis, IN: Wm. B. Burford, 1915.

Royse, Hon. L.W., ed. *A Standard History of Kosciusko County, Indiana.* Chicago and New York: Lewis Publishing Company, 1919.

Sharp, Ronald and Joan. *A History of Syracuse and Environs.* Volumes I, II, III, IV. Syracuse, IN: Sharp's News Service, 1983–1986.

Waldo, C.A., ed. *Proceedings of the Indiana Academy of Science, 1895.* Indianapolis, IN: Wm. B. Burford, 1896.

Visit us at
arcadiapublishing.com

· ·

www.ingramcontent.com/pod-product-compliance
Lightning Source LLC
Chambersburg PA
CBHW050702150426
42813CB00055B/2415